SPLENDID LIVES
and
OTHERWISE

SONNETS OF REMEMBRANCE

Richard Baldwin Cook

SPLENDID LIVES
and
OTHERWISE

SONNETS OF REMEMBRANCE

First Edition 2011

Copyright Richard Baldwin Cook

ISBN 978-1-935538-05-9

Nativabooks.com

Nativa LLC
Cockeysville, MD

Hardcopy available at bookstores
and on line at Lulu.com. Amazon.com
Download through Lulu.com
and
E-book at Google eBookstore

Other books by Richard Baldwin Cook include:

That's What I'm Talking About
All of the Above I
All of the Above II
May it Please the Court

CONTENTS

But if the while I think on thee, dear friend,
All losses are restored and sorrows end.

William Shakespeare
Sonnet 30

Excerpts from Shakespeare's sonnets are taken from *The Sonnets*, William Shakespeare (Penguin Books: New York/ London 1961, 2001), Stephen Orgel, editor

INTRODUCTION

The English sonnet form, made famous by Shakespeare, is the form adopted in this book. Four quatrains and a couplet in iambic pentameter (da DAH, da DAH, etc), with ten syllables to each line. The rhyme scheme is abab cdcd, efef, gg.

A sonnet structure imposes an economy of order upon thoughts one wishes to express. At times, the structure takes over and one puts down an idea that flows toward a rhyme or rhythm. I discovered that I would write, in few words, an idea which had not occurred to me before the sonnet was attempted.

Language controls thought by dictating expression. The sonnet form offers lessons in the way looser forms of written and oral expression, such as essays or conversation also control thought.

On occasion, I have resisted the sonnet form in the interest of expressing a persistent idea. This struggle sometimes leads to a truce, a compromise between the sonnet form and the thought. I suspect this armistice results in a less successful sonnet.

A sonnet is subject to repeated revision. One revisits the sonnet to see if the thoughts cohere and to tighten the form. These sonnets convey facts and impressions based on a completed life. In brief scope, they afford an opportunity for the writer and then the reader to evaluate and to judge both the factual validity and then the impression made by these few lines.

In 2000, shortly after the death of my mother, Elizabeth Taylor Cook, I looked for the first time at a box of family documents she had collected and preserved over a lifetime. The box contained old letters, genealogies, pages from family Bibles and her own notes. Mother had used this material to create a large bowtie genealogy book. I organized this material into three-ring binders, labeled by ancestral surnames. I wound up with over forty binders, with some materials requiring more than a single notebook.

From this material, I wrote two books of family history, one volume devoted to my mother's ancestral lines and the second, to the ancestry of my father. These books, ALL OF THE ABOVE I and ALL OF THE ABOVE II, are available on line and through bookstores and can be consulted for the background of most of the sonnets published here.

Sonnets 1 – 47 relate to my father's ancestors; Sonnets 48 – 106, my mother's. (Except for #72, since we are related not to Jeff Davis but to his wife, Sarah Knox Taylor.)

Considerable stimulating counsel has come to me by way of the book, *LA POESÍA, Hacia la Comprensión de lo poético* by Johannes Pfeiffer (Mexico City: Fondo de Cultura Económico, 2005). The translator of this book, from German into Spanish is Margit Frenk Alatorre, well known for her own original research and writing, who has added Spanish language poetry to the German poems Pfeiffer placed in his original work in 1936. This is an impressive and valuable contribution to Pfeiffer.

Pfeiffer places a high premium on metaphor as an essential component to poetry. Poetry, Pfeiffer wrote, should create layers of meaning for the reader. I have taken Pfeiffer's advice, when I could.

But these poems, written with specific historical events in mind, offer limited opportunities for metaphor. My approach has been to attempt to select a verb or adjective with shades of meaning, leaving the nouns to fend for themselves.

Many of the illustrations are the creations of Leah Fanning Mebane, fanningart.com. See the drawings at sonnets 5, 11, 26, 29, 34, 43, 44, 55, 68, 71, 76, 77, 81, 82, 83.

Beatriz Guzman

My thanks to Beatriz Guzman, granddaughter, for her advice in the preparation of this book.

Bea suggested the book would be better with pictures. No doubt, younger readers will agree.

These poems have been written

with the future in mind

represented by

Nicholas Goodgame Cook

José Oliver Guzman

Isabella Henderson Cook

Beatriz Elizabeth Guzman

But were some child of yours alive that time,
You should live twice – in it and in my rhyme.

William Shakespeare
Sonnet 17

Excerpts from Shakespeare's sonnets are taken from *The Sonnets*, William Shakespeare (Penguin Books: New York/ London 1961, 2001), Stephen Orgel, editor

CONTENTS

REMEMBRANCE OF COOK ANCESTORS

Noah Flood #37
Philadelphia Grayless Carmean #38
Mary Crockett Hawkins #39
Rachel Cook Murphy #40
Robert Jones #41
Sarah Du Bois Van Meteren #42
Sarah Fellows Ireland #43
Susan Farmer Cook #44
Thomas Farmer #45
W.E.B. Du Bois #46
William Cook the First #47

REMEMBRANCE OF TAYLOR ANCESTORS

Archibald Gaines #48
Benjamin Harrison #49
Bridget Walton Taylor #50
Thomas Graves #51
Katherine Gould Parsons Taylor #52
Charles Gent Hedges and Sir Charles Hedges #53
Charles Taylor #54
Charlotte Gamewell Taylor #55
Joseph Parsons #56
Daniel Dudley Mayo #57
Daniel Mayo #58
David Parsons #59
Elizabeth Porter Johnson #60
George Gaines #61
Griffin Bowen #62
Henry Hunt Mayo #63
Isaac Johnson #64
Isaac Morrill #65
Israel Porter #66
Israel Putnam Jr #67
James E. Huey and Sara Crouch Huey #68
James Madison #69
Jane Hedges Baldwin #70
Jane Hedges Baldwin Moore #71
Jefferson Davis #72
Jeremiah Swaine #73

John Gamewell #74
John Maverick #75
John Oliver Taylor, Sr. #76
Jonah Baldwin #77
Joseph Parsons #78
Joseph Putnam #79
Levi Williams #80
Louisa Winston Mayo #81
Marmaduke Moore #82
Mary Baldwin Moore Taylor #83
Mary Bliss Parsons #84
Mary Gye Maverick #85
Mary Putnam Mayo #86
Mary Smith Swaine #87
Myrix Williams #88
Nan Williams Crouch #89
Nathan Parsons Sr. #90
Nicholas Dawson #91
Oliver Swaine Taylor #92
Patrick Henry #93
Robert Doyne #94
Sarah Scott Baldwin #95
Sarah Stebbens Parsons #96
Solomon Scott #97
Thomas Elyot #98
Thomas Moore #99
William Baldwin #100
William Cotton #101
William Harrison #102
William Hathorne #103
William Moore #104
William Stone #105
William Walton #106

1

Abraham Cook
1774-1854

Strong voice raised, father Abraham, for God.
This Shelby County farmer felt the Call.
More natural to keep plowing the sod,
He held back, felt his preparation small.

Abe's piety inherited from Mum.
Welch Baptists two, three generations back.
That, plus New Lights, into the back woods, come.
For sermonizing, Abe Cook, had a knack.

Despite slight reading, Abraham could preach
The Gospel with a voice that carried far.
Revivals' distant sinners Abe could reach.
Throughout the region, Abe Cook was a star.

Abe Cook's career explains Baptist success.
Education replaced by earnestness.

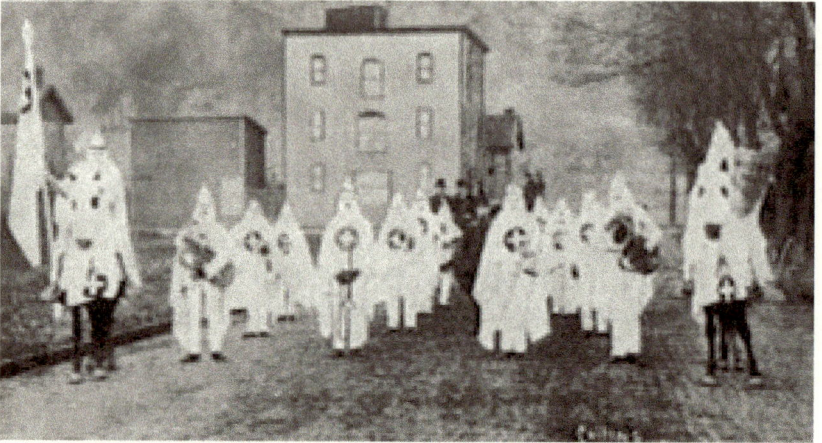

**KKK MARCHING BAND
PENNSYLVANIA, 1906**

2

Addison Cook
1846 – 1871

Beat, Addison an'em, a colored man.
The mail agent, 1871.
This act, to show the power of the Klan,
Benson Station. A'course he had a gun.

Spread all around, he's run off any man,
Looked crooked when they talked of KKK.
Word out on Hiram, shoot him where he stands.
Heard Hiram said A. Cook, the Klan betray.

The road to Bagdad, Hiram laid in wait.
Fired two loads of buckshot at light of day.
Without warning, young cousin met his fate.
Head near blown off. Culprit got clean away.

Hiram on trial, but nothing of it came.
One Moral: if you threaten, best take aim.

3

Agnes Payne Flood
17___ - 17___

Can't recollect the facts about her life.
Housekeeper to the Missus 'til she died.
Young Agnes 'came old John Flood's second wife.
That Agnes bore him six, can't be denied.

When death stole him away, John left much land.
Stole also birthright of the youngest six.
In court, sons of first Missus took command.
Agnes's had no lawyers in the mix.

Her brood went to Kentucky before long.
Began each one a household with a spouse.
Hard, simple frontier living made them strong.
Had no truck with Flood kin back in John's house.

Advice to young women, rich work as maid.
Old man must give a writing 'fore he's laid.

4

Anthony Crockett
1756 - 1838

The Crocketts of old Europe were his clan.
Forced from there, frontier freeholds they did seek.
At Saratoga fought – a happy man:
Brits' cannon and Brits' colors at his feet.

Ant'ony went to Blue Grass, try his turn.
Did well, became there one who would contend.
At arms once more, when Brits new D.C. burn.
In Canada, he took that gun again.

Returned, graced Frankfort's legislative halls.
Sergeant at Arms for decades. Also farmed.
Heroic prototype, when duty calls.
Anthony Crockett served in peace and armed.

His goals were clear and job to do, the same.
Anthony Crockett merited his fame.

ARABELLE AMERICA IRELAND

5

Arabelle America Ireland Dorland
1850 - 1895

They met when Arabelle was bare nineteen.
Her dad would have approved of James' desire.
Matured in Sherman's Blue, much death he'd seen.
Old Abe at war, her father did admire.

They wed in Indiana, then moved east.
First couple in their lines did not jump west.
Raised daughters two, in Lou'ville, 'fore the beast,
of cold and final darkness stilled her breast.

Oh, Arabelle, you died and could not see,
James in his rigid mansion's emptiness
or daughters wed, at least one happily,
or chubby grand babes lean to your caress.

You died too young, no solace could you give,
When son-in-law elected not to live.

6

William F. Cook
1802 – 1850/55

Lucy wed Billy Dick in Thirty-three.
Settled on Shelby land, got from his Dad.
Five children born to this farm family.
Bare twenty years from wedding, Billy had.

Both in their thirties, when these two were wed.
Suggests some diffidence in both their minds.
Their marriage ordinary, all things said.
Bill Dick worked hard; took his sport rough at times.

Annoyed old folks, when he shot pigs for fun.
Drank some, but still, no record of no brawl.
Died just when he might counsel Josh, his son.
Figures in Josh's memoir, not at all.

Quick death mutes your own doings for all time.
Mutes also you to those who come behind.

The Saint Bartholomew's Day Massacre 1576

7

Casper Diller
1696 – 1787

Young Casper Diller, Calvin had his heart.
German Reformed, by French theology.
Land in America! He'd get his part.
This cobbler's dream of wealth, fulfilled would be.

Deutsch speaking Casper Diller, 'fact was French.
His parentage and surname prove that's true.
In P A, he forsook the cobbler's bench,
Advanced himself, as Huguenots did do.

Lived on vast lands near Annville, with his wife.
No, two, because his Anna Barbara died.
By doting heirs, surrounded late in life,
A cruel sectar'an fate, Casper defied.

Fled hostile France, refuged in Germany,
His grandkids fought the Hessians to be free.

8

Catherine Blanchan DuBois
1640 - 1713

Dodged death, Catherine DuBois, by singing psalms.
Dutch so remember in their histories.
Captured by the Minnisink. No qualms,
In killing pris'ners. Still, some mysteries.

Three months their detainee, snows coming soon.
Fierce, hungry Minnisink fired up a blaze.
(To eat their hostages?) Cate tried a tune.
The Minnisink were mightily amazed.

Untied Cate. Sing more psalms, they did implore.
The guided rescuers, too, hear Cate's voice.
Those awestruck Minnisink, awesome no more.
They fled. Devout, devoted Dutch rejoice.

This tale, a super race boldly displays,
A "friendly Indian" his own, betrays.

9

Charity
18_? – 18_ ?

John Farmer's Charity received no praise.
Applause should have been given all the time.
His Charity the Farmer children raised.
His Charity the family larder primed.

His Charity made up the beds and cots.
With silver and china, his table set.
His Charity emptied the chamber pots.
His Charity at his door strangers met.

Such small, essential acts merit acclaim.
Wife dead, his Charity the home fires saved.
But John's Charity goes with no last name.
The common lot of Africans enslaved.

Accustomed to be served, John's Heav'n is Hell.
When he rings, none will answer poor John's bell.

ELLERY FARMER

10

Ellery Farmer
1879 - 1964

Ellery Farmer chronicled his line,
After a life in uniform he'd spent.
Wrote out with wise affection of the time,
Progenitors, their children, forward sent.

Ellery knew the value of firm marks,
On pages noting near forgotten deeds.
To heirs, his scribbles thrilling as the lark's
Dawn trill. Gives hope, the darkest night recedes.

Suppose Ellery left no great estate.
What of this priceless book that all may read?
True wealth, a spiteful fortune does mistake.
His hist'ry, food, new generations feed.

Fine Ellery, dark Farmer cent'ries rent.
His Farmer Family history heav'n sent.

JAMES EMERY DORLAND

11

Ezekiel Dorland
1812 - 1846

Ezekiel died so young, Jim made no cry.
A babe of two, Jim's father not two score.
A two'er cannot know why daddies die.
Forever, Jim draws near to that closed door.

Lucinda raised up EZ's kids, though poor.
Two children died too soon, as EZ had.
Thirteen was Mary, Richard scarcely more.
But little Jimmy Dorland made her glad.

Marched South with Sherman, rebel boys he killed.
Returned. Did well in business. Mother's pride.
A guest in his grand home in Louisville,
In time, Jim placed his mom at EZ's side.

Ezekiel unremembered, nothing done.
Honored by splendid life of James, his son.

JAMES E. DORLAND, USA

**OLD RAG MOUNTAIN
SHENANDOAH VALLEY, VIRGINIA**

12

George Slagle
1761 - 1829

Boy soldier, George, of the exceeding young
Rebellion. Drummer George's adventure
Unrecorded. George yet stands tall among
The noted in his line. Missed indenture

by birth: York County P A. Drummed for men
marching against DER FEIND! Poor German farm
boys. No choice these kids, indentured Hessen
lads. Bad treated at home. Now greater harm

Faced from all points; lined hard against frontier's
Rifles; quartered in sties; sickened by food.
Slop. Ill treated by their own officers.
In numbers died, unmourned, denounced no good.

George drummed into full fire and kept his life.
In Shenandoah, George found peace, not strife.

**"GEORGE SLAGLE
DRUMMER FORMAN'S PA TROOPS
REVOLUTIONARY WAR APRIL 21 1828"**

HOWARD ELLIOTT COOK

13

Howard Elliott Cook
1905 - 1956

Howard, Lost Boy, we know you as our lad.
To Drucy and J F, born in '05.
She sacrificed for you; was only glad,
To do all in her power that you thrive.

Sent you cruising to Europe and to Brown.
You published urgent poems, future bright.
Gay ways for you secured a cap and gown.
Embraced by private friends both day and night.

The Twenties, giddy; Thirties, came the Fall.
Ensnared you, little birdie on a spit.
You fluttered still, wrote poems, acted tall.
L.A., Hawaii, Wake Island seemed a fit.

The War did what the Great Crash could not do.
Four years pris'ner in China finished you.

LOUIS XIV OF FRANCE

14

Jacob Baillet
1641 - 1706

Jacob Baillet, first laborer, then judge.
Alsace, when French Protestants oft' held sway,
From time to time. Their history a smudge.
France drove them out, slipped into disarray.

Pendulant swings first hurt, then helped old Jake.
Died magistrate in 1706.
His children suffered migrants' dire fate.
Forced into Platz; there, future still not fixed.

Grandson Casper took fam'ly 'cross the pond.
Were Lutheran, reformed, it does appear.
Did Casper think him, Grandpa frowned upon?
Not likely. Casper added wealth each year.

Those Huguenots, an energetic bunch.
Best leave them be, or they might eat your lunch.

JAMES E. DORLAND
1844 – 1915
Grandson

15

| James Dorland | Mary Moore |
| 1781 – 1858 | 1 785 - 1869 |

When Jimmy left New Jersey, Ellie cried.
She knew she would not see her boy again.
Brief, stopping in P A, to make a bride,
Jim moved his Mary to Ohio's plain.

They farmed near Fredericksburg, and went to church.
Of their thirteen children, 'bout twelve survived.
None of these kids, the Dorland name besmirch,
Hunt California gold, Dorlands connived.

James, born when George, our Gen'ral raised the torch,
Would live up to the edge of Civil War.
Old Mary saw it from her widow's porch.
John Morgan went to prison near her door.

James Dorland surely loved his own farm best,
In days when Ohio was the Old West.

VAN GAASBEEK / SENATE HOUSE
KINGSTON, NY (1676)

16

Jan Joost Van Meteren
? - 1706

Jan Joost arrived with wife and five on *Vos*
In '62, in Wildwych; that's Kingston.
Oath to the Dutch, then Brits. Competing close,
' Til Will Orange in Windsor had a run.

That set, Jan Joost made money like the rest,
Of the new New Yorkers. For this they'd come.
Old Europe's fights and cultures second best,
To money in the bank. Enlarge that sum!

Judge Jan got property in Jersey, too.
In 1706, went to his grave.
His will proved him American straight through.
Left heirs man, wife, four children, all enslaved.

Strange; freedom, to free colonists, a whim,
Was limited to look alikes, like them.

17

Jean Van Meter
1683 – 1745

He partnered up with Mom, his first land deal.
Jean bought New Jersey pastures; did not stay.
Bought Frederick, then regretted, though a steal.
That town did not exist in Jean's own day.

No job, moved west. Whole life, Jean chased the sun.
Frustrated that that orb set on no towns.
For Shenando' pitched Virgin Gov and won.
His cus' Jost Hite put farmers on those grounds.

Died on a speck of land that little charmed.
Both farm and Jean Van Meter, spot of gloom.
While others settled, Jean said, 'I'll be darned.'
Dutch explorer, a hundred years too soon.

Wanted to buy and sell vast real estate.
For this market to crest, Jean had to wait.

**THE WHIPPING POST
NEW CASTLE, DELAWARE
1896**

18

Jesse Grayless
1733 - 1779

War work of Jesse Grayless noted down.
2nd L T, then 1st, two companies.
He brought wheat to the troops from his own ground.
Patriot, warrior, planter, if you please.

Old Line Soldier from County Caroline.
Owned acreage called "Todd's Venture" in that day.
Jess and Trephena's daughter in her time,
Wed Curt. In young Ohio, were mainstays.

Jess' mother was no bride in '33.
The infant got her name, as she not wed.
Joe Pearson filled her arms with babe Jesse.
She tied to "bublic post," whipped 'til she bled.

Mary Grayless "begat a bastard child"
Who honored name and nation in fine style.

MAYFLOWER

19

John Beauchamp
1585 - 1655

John Beauchamp, moiety in ship *Mayflower*.
Sharp practiced Huguenot, his funds he'd risk.
Control of Pilgrims far outside John's power.
Interminable squabbles, off, John pissed.

"You persecute each other on a whim."
"You purge all those who don't jump to your tune."
'Haps we'll make new adventurers to swim.
We'll pull the plug on these high jinks and soon.

Too late. A new group, better placed and led.
Soon Plymouth, Massachusetts Bay eclipsed.
John, others watched profit from what he's said.
He fumed and fussed in London with pursed lips.

From founding myths, we praise the Pilgrim mind.
At root, they fought and squabbled all the time.

JOHN GOODE FARMER

20

John Farmer
1808 – 1871

John Farmer's harried soul, sad, self-torment.
Convinced himself, was disapproved of God.
For deeds enacted not, endless repent.
Believed himself alive beneath the sod.

No doubt, he harshly troubled his poor wife.
In letters to Kate, pleaded death not call.
His anguish never ended in this life.
His end came with his face turned to the wall.

First Katherine died, left her babes to their lot,
The children mired in vistas of the Fall,
That might have sent their untried minds to rot,
In hells conjured by John their cheerless paw.

Relief eluded John this side his grave,
Might peace have found him had John freed his slave?

OLD MARKET, WINCHESTER VIRGINIA

21

John G Feller
1781 - 1868

Young John G Feller, citizen and vet.
Of 1812. Then his homestead he'd fix,
In Shenandoah, but John G'd not get,
A land grant like the vets of '76.

Not social, yet a joiner was John G,
In iron works, scattered in the Valley round.
Formed wood molds for hot iron poured carefully.
Such toil for food and shelter, John G found.

G after John may not a lone G be.
Gefeller got quick shortened by the clerk.
No matter how recalled in history,
Remembered down his line for clever work.

Drawn South, German homesteaders from P A,
They're found in Shenandoah to this day.

THE LAST JUDGEMENT

22

John Goode
1739 – 1792

Be dipped by Baptists? John Goode thought it queer.
His neighbor told him of their cunning way.
John's folks on Four Mile Creek, a hundred year.
Were Anglican throughout and planned to stay.

The New Lights from up east, he'd not extol.
Of their damnable doctrines, he'd been warned.
They can't rest, its' said. Dip you is their goal.
Truck with such zealous folk, old John Goode scorned.

Felt God convict his soul. Cried his remorse.
Was baptized, John, by "Holy Ghost and fire."
Excitement such, he near fell off his horse.
Began to preach, urge sinners from the mire.

John Goode, sensations heavenly, did feel.
Who can say if these promptings false or real?

23

John Murphy
1752 – 1818

John married Rachel Cook in '74
They roamed, it seems, four colonies and states.
Ensign and then Lieutenant in the War.
In *Kentuck*, for his scruples, John, the fates,

Punished severe; his pulpit, took away.
Like his father, John was Bible-enthralled,
Dirt farmed, delivered sermons on Sunday.
Put Bible against Slav'ry; John was appalled.

Denounced slave-holding quite straightforwardly,
Which meant slave holders, John denounced as well.
The church "excluded" John; belatedly
learned John enrolled them in self-fashioned Hell.

Vindication, John could not live to see,
Horrific, blood-drenched end to slavery.

SHENANDOAH VALLEY HOMESTEAD, 1753

24

Joseph Rentfro
c. 1700 – 1772/76

Was fit, Joe Rentfro's house for Sunday prayers.
To English and their slaves, reader read verse.
King James Bible, not Kings' or Queens' but theirs.
One hundred forty years, blessings and curse,

Flowed over colonists. The K J B,
Its cadences, their phrasings, chants and chimes,
Had marked them plainly English to a tee.
No priest on hand. Were prayers just pantomimes?

The Jew invites the English, self select.
One goal, one law, one Lord, and Him, of Hosts.
In certainty, they saw their paths correct,
By God, the Father, Son and Holy Ghost.

Joseph and Mary Rentfro's practice gave,
Hope to the English, solace to the slave.

25

Joshua Flood
1772 – 1850

Joshua, from Virginey, came out poor.
His Daddy, old John Flood, liked first sons more.
The damn Virginia Highs plain slammed the door.
Josh with Marie lit out, see what's in store.

Bluegrass homestead, worked farm, raised kids, strict
rules:
Keep pigs, horses, work slaves, favor home brew,
No indoor hearth, and absolute: no mules.
Shot dead, hog on the run, a time or two.

Josh Flood, old timey Baptist through and through.
Each wretch must turn to Jesus; says it all.
His heroes John the Baptist, Jackson, too.
Tom Jefferson and the Apostle Paul.

"There ain't no devil I cannot fetch down"
Old Joshua repeats his proverb sound.

JOSHUA FLOOD COOK

26

Joshua Flood Cook
1834 - 1912

Young Joshua Flood Cook had salted down,
All that he learned, for old Joshua's gain.
Fled from the blacksmith's shop clean out of town.
Blue Grass boy in Missouri, made his name.

Built confidence, Unk Noah helped a deal.
To Georgetown College, young Joshua sent.
Broad smile, firm hand, connections made a meal.
Life lessons for this college president.

Survived the war and the dark peace that trailed.
His school survived, when many just sank down.
Denounced the Reconstruction, as he failed,
To question slavery's horrors on the ground.

For Josh, religious zeal the laurel wins.
The zealot enjoys good life with his friends.

27

Katherine Spencer Hawkins Farmer
1814 - 1851

Did Katherine Hawkins know just what she got?
When she brought John Goode Farmer to her side?
She bore his seven children but did not
See them through tender childhood, 'fore she died.

Death wrenched away a babe, then came for Kate.
While shopkeeper John brooded his own end.
Surviving kids, a somber home their fate.
Though sister Sue did lovingly them tend.

Some Farmer kids did fine, their lineage praise.
One died at Shiloh in war John would cheer.
Sue mothered husband; skill from early days.
Kate missed all, died in thirty-seventh year.

Capricious death takes whom and when it will.
All living in all times pay this due bill.

28

Lucas Dorland
1815 – 1897

Got hundred proof of Calvin, mother's milk.
Cold winter, routine worship, to him seemed.
Served pious frontier churches of that ilk.
Grand fiery transformations, Lucas dreamed.

Broke Civil War, Luke would not hold his still.
Heart felt to Luke, all races Jesus Saves.
Saw nation's future harmonize His will.
Enslaved soon to be honored former slaves.

Went to the Carolinas where he taught,
Freed Negroes in new schools he helped create.
Found wealthy donors, whom his vision caught.
An active Gospel Call, Luke's happy fate.

To those slow to aid freed slaves, Luke was curt.
New spring he'd warrant. Winter not revert.

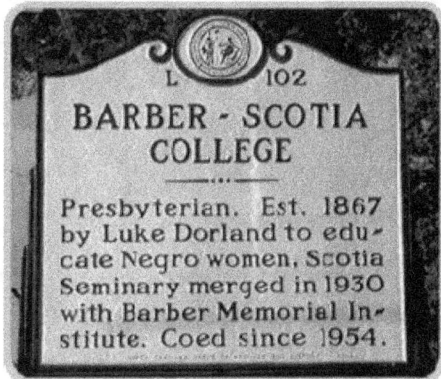

BARBER - SCOTIA COLLEGE

Presbyterian. Est. 1867 by Luke Dorland to educate Negro women. Scotia Seminary merged in 1930 with Barber Memorial Institute. Coed since 1954.

LUCINDA HALEY DORLAND

29

Lucinda Haley Dorland
1818 - 1893

Our Lucinda Dorland, death befriended.
Her father Richard died at thirty-eight.
At six, her plans and dreams all upended.
God did not spare a father for her sake.

Wed Ezekiel; dead at thirty-four.
She then placed two young children in the grave.
Their James alone would live near to four score.
By bargaining with Fate, did James, Lu save?

She'd nothing God might want, God couldn't take.
James went to war and killed, returned a man.
Obtained an education for her sake.
Then James supported her as hoped, not planned.

The US frontier closed the year she died.
But private, inner paths remain untried.

30

Lucy Flood Cook
1802 - 1865

Mom Lucy Cook invoked the one true God,
To make her little boy himself behave.
Old Joshua recalled, she spared the rod.
Acute rebuke: her son she made to pray.

Born in Kentucky in '02, her folk
Were Old Dominion exiles; pioneers.
Deprived of Flood possessions at a stroke;
Granddad John Flood held first wife, sons more dear.

Knew, Lucy, surely, she had married rough.
Her Billy Dick could drink and fire a gun.
Perhaps she turned Bill tender from his tough.
Just as she tempered down her wayward son.

Each mom, the sweet and gentle, perfect saint.
At least that's what sons write, showing restraint.

31

Margaret Cook
1734 - 1797

Marg'ret (Jones?) Cook, devoted and devout.
She raised a clan of Cooks, Southwest V A.
When *Kentuck* opened up, they all set out.
Appears her William Cook died on the way.

In those days, Blue Grass homestead risked your life.
Two sons, two grandsons, killed by the Shawnee.
More deaths averted by each man's brave wife.
They drew blood, made the hunting party flee.

Marg'ret saw her kids baptized, left a will.
She gave to heirs her coin and property.
Transferred a child. Kentucky had instilled,
Virginia's cruel regime of slavery.

The Cooks prayed but were rough, the records say.
Marg'ret would know us if she looked today.

32

Margaret Slagle Fellers
1794 – aft 1843

Mrs. Feller's daughter marries Ireland lad.
Her own folks German, a big family.
Her husband born on this side, like his Dad.
This birth still met strict German pedigree.

The kids come; some wed in the clan, some not.
The lingo's gone away, that's understood.
Their Sarah who wed Martin, said, its rot,
Think Irish husbands don't treat wives too good.

Martin Ireland, not Irish. That's the thing.
From Ulster, folks, where, to saints, they don't pray,
Or sign the Cross or kiss some bishop's ring.
My Martin named for old Luther. OK?

Now, kids, the parents want to keep old styles.
No chance, boys, when young dimples meet young smiles.

OLD AUGUSTA COUNTY VIRGINIA

33

Maria Van Meter
1709 – aft 1795

Maria Van Meter, Dutch French descent.
She married Welch, when she picked Robert Jones.
Both near one hundred years on this orb spent.
From Jersey, southside 'ginia got her bones.

Her mom died very year Maria born.
Is this why she followed her dad around?
He'd move and she'd move, too. Were never torn,
Hearth ties. Felt daddy kept her safe and sound?

They trailed to Maryland. Bob worked with Paw,
As constables in the tall western hills.
Then, Shenandoah, when Dad's itch did gnaw,
And make him shy from cultivated fields.

Down time, as specter Maria displays.
The usual out, when mens has all the says.

MARTIN IRELAND

34

Martin Ireland
1821 – 1904

Was Martin Ireland, Irish? Not at all,
Unless Scotch Irish, does that term define.
Irascible forbearers did install,
In him a domineering cast of mind.

To Sarah Fellows wed, whose inner strength,
Matched Martin's drive to grab life by the throat.
Had nine children, taught each to do and think.
His M.D. status, but small cause to gloat.

In rural Indiana, life was met,
Head on. Their Children learned to make their way,
With assertiveness. Quite high standards set.
A son, M.D, then Gen'ral in his day.

The stamp of what we are and what we do,
Environmental, but ancestral, too.

35

Mary Bondurant Flood
1782 - 1863

Sweet Mary lived to tell her rapt grandson,
Secrets of woodland life with Josh, back when.
Best times, were in their cabin of room, one,
Dirt floor, log walls. Plain bedstead, thought was grand.

Forks poked into the ground, poles laid across,
To catch chinks in the walls, then planks like bars,
Crosswise the poles, then bedding you would toss.
Marie, from this divan, could see the stars.

Josh cut brush, for their mammoth nighttime fires.
Refused indoor cook stove, when they came in.
Sweet Mary said, no more her Josh requires.
Huguenot girl kept house for her young man.

Such discontent! We know we've lost it all,
If we don't go each weekend to the mall.

36

Michael Keinadt
1720 – 1796

This Michael Keinadt, stolid, tetchy man.
When young, began by sending ships to sea,
With merchandise to sell in the new land.
Storm-drowned sister caused inland, Mike to flee.

He farmed, raised many children quite devout.
In P A, lived the balance of his life.
In old age, Mike's kids wanted to move out,
To Shenando', where land and slaves were rife.

With or without complaint, began anew.
Mike may have planned it all. We can't know, now.
His will perhaps surprised more than a few,
Instructing heirs, protect his Nubian Sall.

Life's passions not just ours, relish or rue.
The ones who came before were fevered too.

NOAH FLOOD

37

Noah Flood
1809 - 1873

A credit, in Missouri, to his line.
Flowed this Flood from the Floods of Buckingham,
Virginia, where old John Flood last reclined.
Though English, counseled sons: help Uncle Sam.

Dad moved to Blue Grass. Noah did not stay.
A wagon to Missouri was his choice.
Honored in Baptist lore and history.
Upstanding, wise, preached with a clarion voice.

Shared home and wisdom with young nephew, Josh.
Who fled a Shelby County blacksmith shop.
His father dead, Josh prospects nothing posh.
His downward spiral, Uncle N. did stop.

One puts one's gifts to excellent employ,
When time taken to counsel a young boy.

MERRITTE WEBER IRELAND
1855 – 1954
Great Grandson of
Philadelphia Grayless Carmean

38

Philadelphia Gradeless Carmean
1760 - 1854

Philly was born in Mar'land 'fore the war.
Wed Curtis Carmean in Caroline.
In 1801 lived in Baltimore.
Ten kids. Moved to Ohio, eight or nine.

Daughter, Lizzie was born in 'ninety-eight.
In Ohio, she Stephen Ireland wed.
Steve, like she, from Maryland. Keep this straight:
From Old Line to Ohio, the clans sped.

Liz died in 'forty-eight, Philly lived on.
Knew Ireland great grandkids. For her gave thanks.
She stories, songs and jokes, them rained upon.
Old lady was returned with playful pranks.

"Speak only good of all, alive or dead.
"Take Ol' Scratch. Friends in all ranks," Philly said.

39

Mary Crockett Hawkins
1781 -1856

We choose to think Polly a cheerful child.
Her name gives license, this wish to believe.
Take care imaginings not run us wild.
Some children with a lyric name do grieve.

Her parents were well known and so well thought.
Her dad part of the legislative swells.
More! In the Revolution Daddy fought.
But none of this on family hearth tells.

Wed William Hawkins, raised six girls, one boy.
That girl we trace, left no word of her Mum.
A simple line from Polly we'd enjoy.
But nothing for us but a muted tomb.

Write down a line, a paragraph, a book.
Give curious descendents where to look.

40

Rachel Cook Murphy
1753 - 1832

Rachel Murphy, her progeny bewitch.
Of her, the smallest facts we have, chime true.
Imagination paints her portrait rich.
More faithful than place, date, or time might do.

John went a'revolusing; out of food
At home, she went horseback to distant mill,
Leaving three famished kids in cottage rude.
Heard Ma's voice; opened door to panther's trill.

John still away, food gone and that's a fact.
Our Rachel followed cows, see what cows did,
And what they ate. She then got in the act.
Brought cattle's choice greens home to feed her kids.

'Round hearth, Maw Rachel spoke of long passed day.
Our luck; they wrote out what she had to say.

41

Robert Jones
1696 – aft 1796

Bob Jones, old Wales bred into very bone.
Where he was born, in 1696.
On him and family, the New Light shown.
In Bob's line, Baptist piety was fixed.

Wed a Van Meter girl. Bob's life's pursuits,
Thus set by Jean Van Meter, North Star bright,
Whose daughter followed Jean's slow westward routes.
Upon them, this orb trained both heat and light.

Bob, in Virginia, reached one hundredth year.
Watched generations young, to Blue Grass flow.
Where they were baptized, sang with voices clear,
The hymns of Watts, been taught him long ago.

Ancestor worship – notion we eschew.
Not simple though – they taught us what we knew.

42

Sarah Du Bois Van Meteren
1664 - 1726

Sarah Du Bois, Flanders adaptation.
A Minnisink captive, felt right at home.
Her progeny helped create the nation.
Were guided by example set by Mum.

Born in New York, or rather Amsterdam.
The new one, on the west side of the lake.
Stayed long enough to marry a Dutch ram,
Then bought New Jersey farmland, for kids' sake.

Firm Sarah, looking west with fixèd gaze,
Discussed it all with Jean, her itchy son.
He'd not stay to plow up the Garden State.
Mother taught Jean to pitch, follow the sun.

So Jean did pitch, received substantial grants.
Learned how to, from his parent without pants.

Sarah Fellows Ireland

43

Sarah Fellows Ireland
1829 – 1921

Drummed in the Revolution, granddad George.
Moved west from Shenandoah, left the clan.
In Ohio, parents for her, did forge,
A new start, far from slavery's grasping hand.

Soon, Sarah met her Martin, young man sure,
And confident, he's bound to make a name.
Become a country doc – entrepreneur.
Spent time between the sick and money's game.

Nine children and a household in her care,
While Martin in the wider world would go.
Buried Martin bucolic. She died where?
A town younger than Sarah: Chicago.

Ancestors entitled to be fated.
They lived in a world first they created.

SUSAN FARMER COOK

44

Susan Farmer Cook
1838 – 1890

Sue's somber father pointed her toward God.
As well, her husband, but with humor preached.
Sue's children felt her love but not the rod
Of discipline as she preferred to teach.

Sue stood by Joshua through many trials.
He kept her high in status and in wealth.
She answered him with loyalty and smiles,
Until deaf heaven stole away her health.

Sue died before her youngest son had met,
His Blanche Jeanette, a beauty from the West.
Though strangers, Blanche helped reach the goals Sue set,
For Cecil Cook, who preached above the rest.

Two more wives Josh, her husband would procure,
But Susan Farmer made his line secure.

YORKTOWN, VIRGINIA
SEVENTEENTH CENTURY

45

Thomas Farmer
1586/94 - ?

Tom Farmer to Virginia coast right quick.
'Haps hoped few knew the reasons for the move.
Recusants in Old England, though not thick.
His families' troubles there undo him prove.

First settlers enough worries, just survive.
Good Tom brought gifts and talents wanted there.
Made leader in the Burgesses. Alive,
After the massacres killed numbers fair.

Our Tom slips into shadows near the end.
Cannot be traced, his destiny's details.
It's known he married. Tom's descendents wend,
Down their unique nation's historic trails.

To Thomas Farmer, lift a glass who can:
Recusant. Adventurer. Fam'ly Man.

W.E.B. DuBOIS

46

William Edward Burghardt Dubois
1868 – 1963

W.E.B. DuBois, last angry man.
Dutch-African his heritage. So run,
Comments mouth to mouth, records hand to hand.
His scholarship like bullets from a gun.

Felt endless race insults like blows or fire.
Knew peace would come, if comes, down prolonged roads,
Whose ends he would not reach, 'fore he's retire,
Into shadows, when slaves laid down their loads.

Never a slave, but Harvard Ph.D.
Visions of schooled elite, ever hearkens.
Too patient, Booker T; verbose, Garvey.
DuBois' faith: "world brightens as it darkens."

If fury by itself could freedom ring,
Our cousin Will is Moses! All would sing.

NORTH AMERICAN ORCHID

47

William Cook
c 1720 – c 1784

In Blue Ridge foothills, young Will Cook inclined,
Conduct prayer services. Was Anglican.
In land speculated, much of the time.
Made Justice of the Peace, that kind of man.

Boone opened Keentuck up. Will's kids rushed in.
He sold off what he owned, to boost their dreams.
Big sendoff William got, from friends and kin.
Left for the West, died on the way, it seems.

They did the best they could, Will's Blue Grass clan,
Left Franklin County; Shelby offered more.
They missed their patriarch's sure, guiding hand,
Few heirs were wealthy, some middling, some poor.

From London slums or of Virginia clay,
Marked deep the earth, did Will Cook in his day.

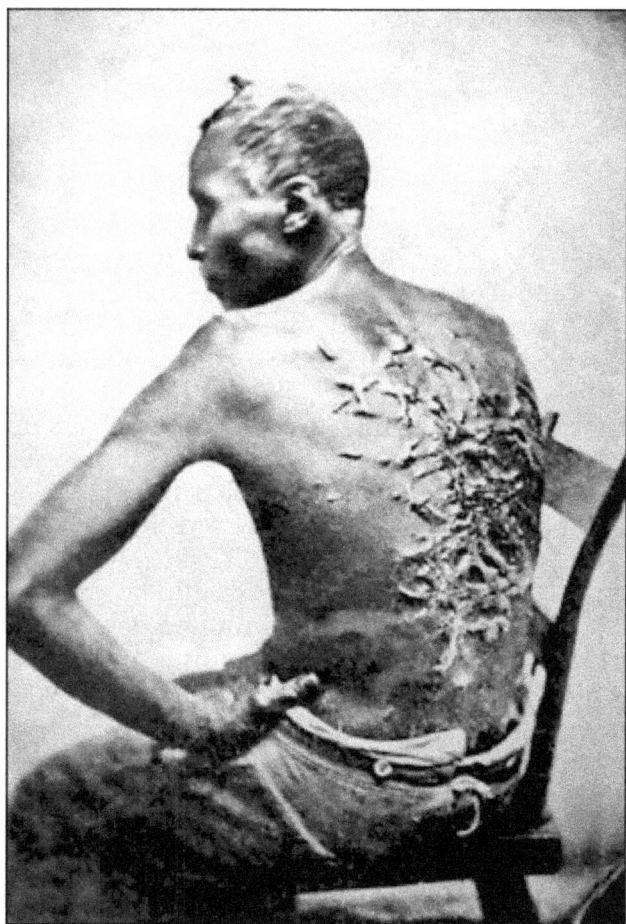

48

Archibald Gaines
1808 - 1871

His only enemy, the river wide.
So, when Marg'ret grabbed up her kids and risked,
Ohio ice flows, into freedom stride,
Both old and young alike, Archie was pissed.

He trap'em up in Cinci, went to court,
With lots of help from young bloods on horseback.
Admitted that the kids were his, of course,
Slaves, runaways, all property in fact.

Marg'ret killed her babe. Closed those eyes so blue.
Knew daughter'd not be free upon this earth.
Mother not tried for murder. Judge, well knew,
Father would tend to her, for all she's worth.

He raped her as he pleased. That was the way,
To handle feisty gals, back in the day.

49

Benjamin Harrison
? – 1808

Ben Harrison, not one to let the grass
Grow under feet, which kick, as well as walk.
In Pennsylvania, could punt British ass.
And did. Preferred it to a civil talk.

Impatient or just steady on? Who knows?
Out in Blue Grass, beyond the damn frontier,
Ben was the man knew what to do. It shows.
The county named for Ben, made all that clear.

He started up a school, then moved again.
The Mississip he crossed. Hit Spain. Last trek.
Spick Gov there, made him laugh, our Benjamin.
Said: You can stay, long as you genuflect.

Today, we ruminate 'bout peace and love.
'Cause guys like Ben gave enemies the shove.

50

Bridget Walton Taylor
1746 – 1851

Grand Bridget Walton Taylor, mom and wife.
For word of her, the past has closed its doors.
When young, the loom no doubt encompassed life.
Once wed, that loom traded for farmwife chores.

Great granddad to Cambridge; son, two degrees.
These men, a kindly Heaven looked upon.
Was Heaven that gave guys their apogee?
Or women, men in charge have trampled on?

A democratic system adds but slow,
Including the excluded in its reach.
The women only recent gains can show.
This, Bridget's anonymity, does teach.

Resentment causes us, Bridget to cheer?
That we are headed backwards, is the fear.

Nicotiana Tabacum.

51

Thomas Graves
? - by 1637

Cap Thomas Graves' career went up in smoke.
That was the plan. Tobacco good as gold.
Slave empire they set up in but a stroke,
Tabacum 'long with people, bought and sold.

Cannot turn hours left and get it right.
Lung cancer and mass rape our heritage.
Does Tom in Heaven sit up late at night?
Or like the rest of us, just hit the fridge?

Cap Tom in Jamestown. Early on that ground.
Decisions made killed millions then unseen.
A total condemnation is unfound.
This Tom, a Tom come later did redeem.

If lauded by our peers is why we try,
Then Thomas Graves and Jefferson a tie.

52

Catherine Gould Parsons Taylor
1791 – 1865

Cath'rine Gould Parsons, surnames nobly ranked,
Should Old England and royal rules pertain.
But father and grandfather both were thanked.
New England freed and never ruled again.

A patriot daughter, worthy help-mate,
Cate equal to the good man she sustained.
This doctor, teacher, preacher helped create,
America, from homes Catherine maintained.

They moved from their New England, South and West
Cared for the sick, taught boys, and preached the Word.
She lived to see her Revolution crest
In bloody banishment of slavery's scourge.

Cath'rine Taylor, by progeny ranked best,
A vital, free nation, her grand bequest.

SWEEDISH BUILT HOUSE
DOVER, DELAWARE
18TH CENTURY

53

Sir Charles Hedges
1640 - 1712/14

Charles Gent Hedges
? - 1730

Sir Charles Hedges, sec'tary to Queen Anne.
His slighted son, Charles Gent, never knighted.
Son Joe, to Monacacy, Maryland.
In son Jonah, Joe's brief life requited.

This lineage long, from Normans to *Keentuck*.
Mom of Jonah was combo Swede and Fin.
All been tracked with care, no one ran amuck.
If then this line's not clear, begin again.

Jane Hedges Baldwin, lady in K Y.
Rummaged London solicitors, around.
Looking for true heirs; line in England died.
Blind Lady Jane remained heiress unfound.

Find money, lotto win or inherit.
Await lightning strike, or work! You ferret.

CHARLES TAYLOR

54

Charles Taylor
1819 - 1897

Charles Taylors' gifts undone by private ires.
Talent and high intelligence his wealth.
A babe whose birth might merit angel choirs,
Betrayed by grim antagonism's stealth.

Art, Science, Académe signaled his worth.
His father set the mark for selfless love.
To win doomed heathen souls, Charles crossed the earth.
A fisted hand he shaped inside that glove.

Found lovely Charlotte, yellow Jessamine pride,
In time to aide her state and region raise,
Arms 'gainst the land for which forefathers died.
To keep slaves slaves, Charles mortgaged his best days.

Some quite delightful souls cheered Secession.
Charles' Lost Cause mixed desolate depression.

CHARLOTTE GAMEWELL

55

Charlotte Gamewell Taylor
1828 - 1910

The trials of Charlotte Taylor without end.
Into a zealous Methodism born.
Her father John, Asbury's sometime friend.
The slavish South, her early years did form.

John Wesley damned their system, it is true.
But Asb'ry's census showed the White's would save,
His long life's work, so Francis not reprove,
The Methodist enslavement of the slave.

Young Charlotte wed for prominence and love,
We trust, a scholar-doctor. Life unfurled
In China, then the South. But heaven above,
Is where she seeks babes buried 'cross the world.

Firm Charlotte Gamewell Taylor, noble wife.
Charles purchased his career with Charlotte's life.

CHARLOTTE GAMEWELL TAYLOR

This image reproduced courtesy of the Connecticut Valley Historical Museum, no reproduction or exhibition without permission

CHILDHOOD HOME OF MARY BLISS
FUTURE WIFE OF JOSEPH PARSONS
SPRINGFIELD, MA

56

Joseph Parsons
1620 - 1683

A Pilgrim boy, who founded large cities.
Selectman, surveyor, fine tavern owned.
By cheating tribes, added wealth. No pity's
For them found in Joseph, though he bemoaned,

Hurled charges against his wife. A witch, they said.
First suit then counter suit, 'til prosecute.
Long months in jail; her neighbors wished her dead.
Bare body inspected. Thus prostitute,

All law. Serene, Marie, own best witness.
Was vindicated. Did this twice to her.
Old Pur'tan code, toxic, most now attest:
Denounce abuses, then in them, concur.

Cornet Joe Parsons' life mirrors it all.
Invoke God, predatory wealth, then Fall.

DANIEL DUDLEY MAYO

57

Daniel Dudley Mayo
1843 - ?

"There is but little consolation then,
In your hour of grief." Dan ID'd the Thief,
When death had taken brother-in-law Ben.
Dan Dudley Mayo wrote his non-belief,

To older sister, 'Rilla Moore, up home.
Dan left Kentucky not long after war,
Had sundered his society. The dome
Of Rockies, pulled young bucks there by the score.

Dan had no faith in God, but 'Rilla did.
Economy's where Daniel placed his trust.
In Colorado, no one fought to rid,
The state of slavery, system of disgust.

Dan Mayo, good ol' southern boy it's true.
Moore should have left with Dan, began anew.

Paul T. Mayo Home, c. 1920
100 Humboldt Street, Denver

HARVARD COLLEGE 1770

58

Daniel Mayo
1771 - 1838

His dad, well known and liked and poor and dead.
Dan, Harvard man, in his own self invest:
Leave Boston home, take paths anew where led,
Rebellion's victory, the opened West.

Into Ohio, with the Putnam clan.
In Belpre courted Mary, pretty thing.
Did big shot Putnams overbear our Dan?
Great riverine highway, these two did bring,

To young Kentucky, frontier's very edge.
Posted the mail in Newport thirty years.
Bought, sold land and people. To Dan allege,
Their freedom. Was immune, Dan, to their tears.

Dan Mayo, John Q. Adams' Harvard chum.
Divergent paths, divergent futures come.

59

David Parsons
1680 - 1743

Our Dave was raised in priv'lege and hopes high.
Both parents well respected all around.
A Harvard grad in 1705,
Dave Parsons was ordained a cleric sound.

A Malden, Mass. tenure had proved his keep.
The elders in Leicester had taken note.
He was then called to pastor there the sheep.
He went expecting to enlarge his scope.

The sheep, wolves proved, around his lonely manse.
The promised large support was just a game.
Into the local court the parties danced.
Lost, David, salary and his good name.

If from his grave Dave us advise, he should:
Insist not the church give you firewood.

60

Elizabeth Porter Johnson
1610/11 - 1683

Young, orphaned Betty crossed from home alone.
Her granddad, Robert, Tudor priest had been.
Led prayers when Anglican bright sun had shone.
Granddaughter saw need to begin again.

High church consensus crashed soon as she left.
In Massachusetts Bay, that church no hope.
Beth rich in fam'ly, if in faith bereft.
Could be, cared not a fig for alter smoke.

Were wed near forty years, Isaac and Beth.
Ike killed in poor King Philip's Great Swamp fight.
Command placed in old man, how desperate.
Faced colonies, extinction, endless night.

Often alone, girl child in world of men.
Pick one. Accommodate. Alone again.

UNDERWORLD

61

George Gaines
1764 - 1845

"Can you feel or find heart to pray for me?"
Pastor records George Gaines shrill, stricken cry.
'Haps wilderness redemption mimicry.
Claim Baptist preachers, throngs so testify.

George first in his Gaines clan wend Blue Grass way.
Founded a church or three, confounded Hell.
George with his Susan Graves, from Virgin's clay.
Boone County architecture pleased them well.

His soul endangered terrors did abate.
George dunked, was made new Christian then and
there.
Jesus his Savior, Railroad, Interstate,
Greenback, TV, Babe Ruth, Electric Chair.

On Sabbath, soul examine opportune.
' Fore football, cable, visits to the moon.

THATCHED ROOFED COTTAGE, WALES

62

Griffin Bowen
c 1600 – c 1675

First Griffin Bowen came and then went back.
The annals his incentives don't record.
Wales, Massachusetts, London find his track.
'Haps Bay State realty Welch men can't afford.

His line traced back to son of Norman Will.
But only if the bastard child we count.
We do. Then forward in time, thanks to skill,
Of family 'storians, whose tales we mount.

Old Griff left progeny this side the pond.
You know this from the quatrain you just read.
Son, Henry fought in Great Swamp Battle. Won.
Lived ninety years in two Woodstocks, then dead.

Life seems a sad and dower wail with tears.
Surprises when a grinning Muse appears.

**DUNKER CHURCH AFTER THE BATTLE OF
ANTIETAM, 1862**

63

Henry Hunt Mayo
1810 - 1877

Knew Henry Hunt, his father's standards high.
From up east, Dan, with Harvard accolade.
No school such like for Henry; that's the why:
His letters learned at home, then found a trade.

Dry goods and milling wood, fair, solid work.
Louisa's happy hearth; no grounds to roam.
Much laughter, fun and pranks, the pleasant perk,
To all who visited this Mayo home.

Fates turned on Henry Hunt, when bitter war,
Divided friends, unseated Joy, his muse.
Feared sons forced to supplant the dead encore,
Sent them away; their forfeit he refused.

His wood lot burned, H. H. did pay a cost.
Dan's son quick figured out, Lost Cause was lost.

ATTACKING THE WAMPANOAG FORT

64

Isaac Johnson
1610 – 1675

Our Isaac Johnson's promised grant of land
Went to another, though he did his best.
Gratuity, sworn his by upraised hand
On Dedham Plain, when gathered with the rest.

They marched against the Wampanoag, who's hid,
In their stark swamp refuge, man, woman, child.
Tradition tells, quite well militia did.
In fact, against this foe, some men went wild.

Isaac commanded a green troop he'd raised.
Bad wounded at the entrance of the fort,
In hand to hand combat, much later praised,
For bravery 'gainst the Indian cohort.

Elizabeth was widowed and her ire
Was heightened 'cause he died from friendly fire.

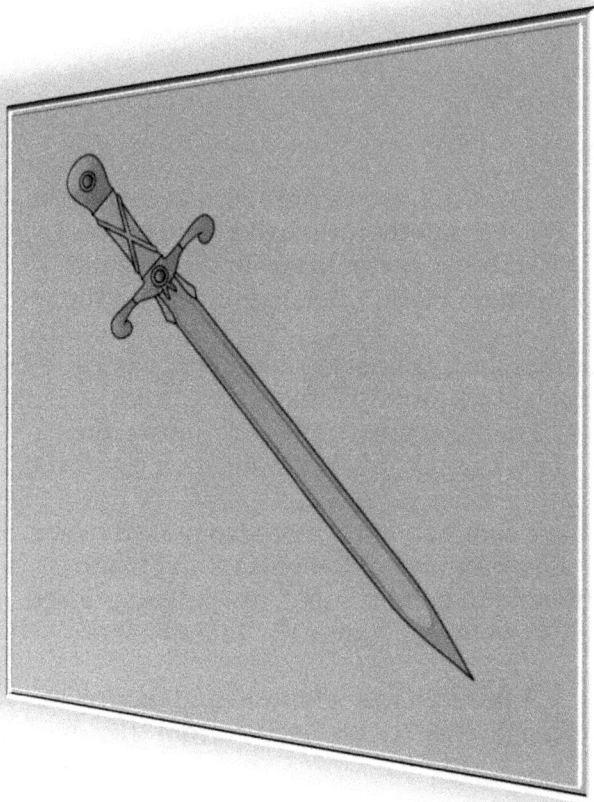

65

Isaac Morrill
c 1587 – 1661

From London Isaac Morrill early came,
By good ship, *Lion,* 1632.
With freeman's voting status, he would tame,
Hard metals as all blacksmiths used to do.

In Roxbury, M A, got two estates.
"Auchmuty" and "Fox Holes" his holdings called.
In Isaac's fine home visitors might gape,
At all the weapons he hung on his wall.

Three swords, a fowling piece, a courselet,
A pike, a half-pike, belts of bandoleers.
These items his descendents proud to get,
Pursued the blacksmith's trade for many years.

An English 'smith with pride, his status claims.
Few own two grand estates, with funky names.

66

Israel Porter
1643 - 1706

Stout Israel Porter, yet remembered well.
He fought the witch hysterics, Salem town.
Worked hard to free defendants 'fore the knell
By prosecutors tolled, in death resound.

Brave Israel failed. Grotesquely, neighbors died,
Pressed under stone or hanged as Satan's tools.
Accusers late repented and some cried,
In church. Confessed they'd acted perfect fools.

Israel himself risked death. When proven right,
Lived, saw triumphal Puritanism wane.
A system which had ushered in the night,
Of bigotry, earned popular disdain.

Foul Plymouth prejudice, most sad to say,
Died not with victims killed in Israel's day.

FARMERS' CASTLE
BELPRE, OHIO

67

Israel Putnam Jr
1738 - 1812

Israel Putnam Jr took his main chance,
On Muskingum River, beyond P A.
That Putnams went to there, no happenstance.
Close plans, Act of Congress, deaths on the way.

Chartered a new state, slave's power exclude.
Ohio made for all who would breathe free.
Transplants from old Virginia they'd include.
Some White Virginia folks hated slav'ry.

Israel and cousin Rufus did it right.
They organized new towns down to the ground.
The ones who followed them were just as bright.
Build schools and yes, protected ancient mounds.

Worship with them? Pur'tans, they'd sure refuse.
The Putnam clan put lib'rals in the pews.

SARA CROUCH & JAMES HUEY

68

James Addison Huey   &   Sara Crouch Huey
1862 – 1961   1861 – 1956

They found each other young, never to part.
Farm kids; his folks from Big Bone, hers, Glencoe.
In Union, life together made a start.
No other place on earth would please them so.

Away to college for two weeks, went James.
He missed too sore his *Kentuck* family home.
Sara's intense allure has many names.
It's love, he said, from her he'd never roam.

Three Children: Joseph, Gaines and daughter Nan.
Depression fortunes, their slight fortune rent.
Fate took their Gaines, then joy, from household, banned.
Mended. Near hundred earthly years each spent.

Fame, love 'tween James and Sara, did not grace.
Affection, fickle fortune not efface.

JAMES MADISON

69

James Madison
1751 - 1836

Remembered ill as President too meek,
He let the city burn. James got it right.
Majorities, he knew, can crush the weak;
Tri-partite systems balance useful might.

James Madison, reliable and wise,
He purposed our Republic, made it great.
His system stands before unseeing eyes,
Most excellent, since Hellas met its fate.

The best of his career not what's best known.
White House service, Britannic war again,
Has cousin's grand bequest not clearly shown?
The Constitution, nation's finest friend.

Jim's greatest gift any forefathers gave.
The shadow on it - nothing to the slave.

OLD AUGUSTA CABIN, 1700s

70

Jane Hedges Baldwin
1752 – aft 1785

My Maw she never said how he'd do me.
Ju'know? I din't know nuthin, nut' a'tall.
Hurt so! Swear, thought he's go'ng clear through me.
He's older than my paw! They talked an' all.

A'right after a while. He's good man. Why,
Good on the farm. Good with the kids, with me.
We just fine. But I did know this. He'd die.
Was old! Alone with babies, I'd sure be.

Things worked out good, I guess I would agree.
I schooled my boys, we kept the farm an' all.
Out in Ohio, say, they's mean and free.
Please me, indeed, go see'm, come next Fall.

My sons, they stay or go, free like they Dad.
My girls' mens they runs things, for good or bad.

JANE HEDGES BALDWIN

71

Jane Hedges Baldwin Moore
1809 - 1893

Jane, posed with kittens, a fine portrait made.
The artist, father brought to their grand home.
Despite her dad's fierce love, the fates weren't stayed.
The age portrayed reached not five of Jane's own.

Jane married M.D. Moore, excellent man.
She bore him ten in Covington K Y.
Protected by investments, not with land.
Raised orphans after theirs began to die.

The Civil War came to, then through, their door.
Did Marma put his money in the ground?
Locked up for bold opinion, nothing more.
Blind, widowed Jane saw yonder Marma's crown.

Jane, blesséd in the men her did adore,
Paw Jonah Baldwin, then Pappy Duke Moore.

JANE HEDGES BALDWIN MOORE

JEFFERSON DAVIS

72

Jefferson Davis
1808 – 1889

Jeff Davis, was no cousin to admire,
Worked to undo what Madison had done.
Another cousin, whose Presidency dire
Did not reflect his fame, though justly won.

Jeff bet against the future for the past.
Bad bargains made, with slavers of his day.
He should have known their system could not last.
To mortgage Jimmy's system, blood would pay.

Two Presidents, their Presidencies twinned,
As failures; measurements later applied.
Jeff Davis' fell never to rise again.
James' efforts live as though he never died.

Stones skimmed on water ripples make. So, Jim
Said: join concentric interests, not whim.

PURITANS GOING TO CHURCH

73

Jeremiah Swayne
1643 – 1710

Firm Jeremiah Swayne first M.D. shown,
In his line in New England. Moment seized.
Selectman, Justice of the Peace, saw bone.
Promoted public order; cured disease.

Jerry and Mary, couple good to know.
Fine family, were reputable, sound.
He marched with the militia, records show.
His soldier's skills essential, Jerry found.

Took up arms in the Narragansett War.
Lieutenant in Sam Appleton's comp'ny.
Was wounded in the taking of the fort.
Lived to tell tales to grandkids on his knee.

Doc Jeremiah Swayne, the kind of man,
Helped his country on its young feet to stand.

**HOME OF GREEN HILL
LOUISBURG, NC
MEETING PLACE
METHODIST ANNUAL CONFERENCE
1785**

74

John Gamewell
1756 – 1827

John Gamewell, old school mariner, at sea.
From Nassau to the colonies, he plied.
Made Methodist by Francis Asbury.
Forsook the sails, preached Jesus crucified.

In Carolinas, John took ship anew.
From green hills to the coast, John anchor marks.
Evangelist, preaches to all or few.
The cap is Christ, crude pulpits are the barks.

Of John, said, he regretted his career,
Ship slaves into their brutal southern fate.
If so, one word from Asbury we'd hear,
Instructing Methodists to free their slaves.

The backward glow invites us all to see,
The phantom champs of slaves, not slavery.

PURITAN HOMES

75

John Maverick
1578 – 1635/6

Years preaching in old Devonshire proved stale.
John Maverick gathered with sectaries brave.
Joined Winthrop, to America they sailed.
With visions of great throngs, their souls to save.

A temperament more placid than some others.
Health failing even as he left the boat.
Brought peace between the fighting two gov'nors.
Dorchester town by-laws John Maverick wrote.

The fate of John's new start he could not know.
His progeny in thousands beyond count.
In our day lights of Boston City show,
On practices John Maverick would denounce.

To Puritans, conformity the game.
To non-conformists Maverick gave the name.

JOHN OLIVER TAYLOR, SR

76

John Oliver Taylor, Sr
1862 – 1922

John Taylor was a charmer with a flaw.
Sardonic, sense of humor, gentle heart.
His kids loved him, and Minnie most of all.
With Barley-corn, John got an early start.

When they wed, John and Min both mid twenty.
He moved his wife into his parents' home.
A parsonage, where were eyes aplenty,
Watched every move, together or alone.

Their first ten years were Heaven, Minnie said.
By then, all John's big plans for them played out.
His sons would find him stumbling 'round, half dead.
His drinking turned her hopes into a rout.

Her life with John, Minnie appraised this way,
Penned in a letter, "sorry was the stay."

JONAH BALDWIN

77

Jonah Baldwin
1777 – 1864/5

Young Jonah came alone but well prepared,
To prairie Springfield, Oh, 'bout eighteen-four.
An Anglican, drover and surveyor,
He opened up a tavern and held court.

Not long 'fore Sarah Scott had caught his eye.
They wed when she was not above fifteen.
Childbirth most likely caused this child to die.
Leaving small ones to Jonah's harsh regime.

He took another wife and raised them all.
Food, shelter, clothing, books, them to be read.
He'd met the great Tecumseh, watched him fall.
A people unprepared, a nation's dread.

The skills that such as Jonah Baldwin brings,
The gifts that made White prairie men be kings.

JONAH BALDWIN

HOME OF JOSEPH PARSONS
Built by his father
Cornet Joseph Parsons, c 1657
Northampton, MA

78

Joseph Parsons
1647 – 1729

When young, he marched and fought, King Philips War.
When old, again, militia service called.
J P, the last, in the old English form.
At eighty-two he died, acclaimed by all.

Selectman, oft selected Judge beside.
To Boston many times to pass the laws.
Sawmill and grist interests ranged Joseph wide.
Both lawyer, businessman, high income draws.

Mother on trial two times for witchery.
Joe did not, for this cause, shun church or town.
With firmer hand than that of you or me,
Persisted and assisted all around.

Joe mulls his works in dark hours 'fore the dawn.
Works' adjunct: keep those witching fools full gone.

ON TRIAL FOR HER LIFE

79

Joseph Putnam
1669 – 1724

Joe Putnam fine inheritance received.
Since favored, father Tom, his second wife.
The Holyoke kids round smaller fires did grieve.
Bequest did separate them from good life.

In Salem, wealthy Joseph not deceived,
Or awed by foolish Magistracy threats,
Directed at witches, or so perceived,
'mong Salem poor and some female misfits.

Objected, Joe, to terror inflicted.
When harsh, false accusations boldly made.
Neighbors he knew well, wrongly depicted,
Witches. Were mere dissenters and afraid.

He, Joseph, and his wife's dad fought as one.
Praised Israel in the naming of his son.

**JOSPEH PUTNAM HOME
SALEM, MA**

LEVI WILLIAMS

80

Levi Williams
1794 – 1860

Old Levi Williams, honored – then denounced.
Vet'ren, War Number two against the Brits,
And Black Hawk War. But then, the Mormons pounced,
Hurled insults. On this sideline, no one sits.

In Illinois, this Baptist pulpiteer,
Was deemed a valued leader of home guards.
Reviled as drunken brutish man to fear,
Levi, dead now, when answer would be hard.

In Mormon hist'ry Levi Williams hissed.
These sources emit unrestrainéd rage.
On trial was he, for killing Joseph Smith.
Acquitted quickly in trial quickly staged.

His-story, writ, they say, by those who win.
But also take their shot, the next of kin.

LOUISA WINSTON MAYO

81

Louisa Winston Mayo
18_? – 18_?

Louisa Winston Mayo 'deed recalled,
Her family's well earned patriotic fame.
The Battle of King's Mountain, most of all,
Where vict'ry gave a fine town half its name.

Louisa and Henry did Mayos raise,
In Newport, where the fates, two rivers set,
In deep channels. Assign here blame, there praise,
For shallow deeds. The Deep's no such regret.

Takes all, churns all, cleans all, in fine, long flows.
A tranquil, happy home, the children knew.
To this hearth its reflection, water shows.
Like Henry and Louisa's – all too few.

To raise up children, love counts more than wrath.
To train those children right, you gotta laugh.

MARMADUKE MOORE

82

Marmaduke Moore
1808 – 1883

Near Cynthiana, born on father's farm.
Home schooled. His folks refused to raise a fool.
Knew what he learned from books would do no harm.
Commodities Duke traded; income spool.

Soon wealthy by the standards then applied.
In thousands out thousands, Marma's routine.
The gloom for M D Moore, the ones who died.
Five of nine of his children; sum obscene.

Replaced them with the orphans of dead sibs.
Pap's home where children's fears were kept at bay.
The War kicked aging Marma in the ribs.
For his Lost Cause opinions, locked away.

Pap Duke knew life and death at best and worst.
Blows somewhat deflected when fam'ly's first.

MARY BALDWIN MOORE

83

Mary Baldwin Moore Taylor
1863 – 1936

To honey, Minnie Taylor, not like flies,
Did draw the local wags up to her door,
Because of her bright looks or fetching eyes?
No. She'd say things they had not heard before.

Quick, Minnie'd snap out a sharp opinion.
On matters local, state or far afield.
Sure, she was the queen of her dominion.
When she made up her mind, Minnie'd not yield.

Her mother warned her; don't you pick a drunk.
At twenty-five, John asked her; she said yes.
Then, lots of kids, no income; she was sunk.
Why Minnie stayed with John, we can but guess.

Retorts from Min, her momentary flight,
From harsh, bleak day, and dreaded lonely night.

MARY BALDWIN MOORE TAYLOR

ACCUSED OF WITCHCRAFT

84

Mary Bliss Parsons
1628 – 1712

Twice Goody Parsons charged with vile witchcraft.
Were "jealous," court records, neighbors betray.
Dragged Mary from her home to court 'fore daft
Charges dismissed; she boldly had her say.

Came with Bliss parents, sixteen thirty five,
Wed Joseph Parsons ten years after that.
Son, killed by Narragansett, she alive.
On Mary's plans for him, misfortune spat.

In England, should'a stayed, onlookers say.
Forgetting that Bliss fortunes there, not grand.
Her grandfather and father, to this day,
Recalled, imprisoned, deprived of their land.

Not misremembered Pilgrims, brother band.
Against women was raised an angry hand.

85

Mary Gye Maverick
c. 1580 – aft 1660

Did Mary Gye descend from Charlemagne?
God knows, might say a Puritan divine.
Like husband John, a man bold to made plain,
That Calvin's theories shaped his somber mind.

From England they moved out; could not conform.
Was this move foreordained like Mary's line?
God knows, they fought against high churchly norm.
In Massachusetts, John's health soon declined.

Widowed Mary, life split between two shores,
She likely dismissed thoughts of ancestry.
God knows, her neighbors raised flintlocks and more,
To cut the native line root, branch and tree.

We're proud when genealogies prove long.
God knows, the first Indian lines are gone.

OLD NEWPORT, KY

86

Mary Putnam Mayo
1773 – 1838

Did Mary Putnam truly want to go?
Connecticut farm and town life, her world.
Harsh trek itself was filed with death and woe.
Some dozens killed before state flag unfurled.

Think, hunting up adventures she embraced.
In castle near Belpre, she would not stay.
Was courted by a swain whose turn out graced,
The further frontier, down Kentucky way.

She Daniel Mayo wed, no backward glance.
They owned nothing they did not build or make.
Newport, this Up East couple did enhance.
They taught their kids, do all for fam'ly's sake.

The riddle: to severe frontier they went.
Solved: worthy, improved lives their children spent.

87

Mary Smith Swayne
1648 – aft 1714

Determined, Mary Swayne wed at sixteen.
Her mother, Catherine by then two years dead.
Her widowed dad, had followed the routine,
Wed Mary Bill, eighteen, brought her to bed.

Two teenage girls, one daughter, and one wife,
One roof, one man, the husband and father,
When said, 'Mary come here,' could lead to strife.
Both Mary Smiths, this moniker bother.

Young Mary, John Smith's child, from home did go.
Picked Jeremiah, fit Reading suitor.
Jeremy Swayne might need a spouse to show.
He twenty-one, unwed, faced pros'cutor.

The Pilgrims planned it all from death to born.
Teenagers getting married, their firm norm.

MYRIX JOSIAH WILLIAMS

88

Myrix Williams
1811 – 1897

Myrix Josiah Williams, tall, aloof.
Welsh Merricks and Williamses, stand behind.
Tiny Glencoe, K Y offers the proof,
The smallest anchor, largest bark will bind.

Legislator, long Magistracy post,
Large crops, grand home, the finest riding horse.
Leisured breakfast; he read the *Journal* close.
Life warranted, sustained by slaves, of course.

Three wives, ten children, Grand Masonic rank.
Admired greatly, Myrix, by many men.
His eminence increased before it sank.
Took sides against his country. Did not win.

Acknowledge ancestry with due respect.
But proffer admiration circumspect.

89

Nan Williams Crouch
1843 – 1923

Kentucky Universe, yours from the start.
Glencoe your world, stern Myrix Williams' home.
Your mother, Junietta in a star.
Not otherwise, died long before you'd grown.

Was yours, Nan, Myrix' slave embellished seat.
Their last toils to your generation gave.
You, former fettered, met on Glencoe street.
Not otherwise, half 'mancipated slave.

You raised your kids in war be'raveged land.
Old universe gone. Missed unmissed the same.
Joy ride to West Coast, surfers saw, first hand.
For this, Dutch, English, Huguenots, here came.

Nan Williams Crouch, a bridge from there to where.
Old lady, mending socks, rocks in her chair.

90

Nathan Parsons Sr.
1721 - 1806

Nate grew into a solitary strength.
His recluse father raged and cursed his fate.
Cup of despond, young Nathan's only drink.
Soon married, from the dower hearth did break.

A farmer and a frontier fighter, he.
Nate's inner life molded by father's ire.
Protected from the French, his Colony.
Though his numb stare caused silence round the fire.

Late decades, Nathan's help was sought once more.
He answered, fought, again made quite a name.
Is honored in his family's folklore.
Nate's cheerless early life, he overcame.

Remembered by the Parsons, soldier true.
A sorry childhood, did not Nate undo.

**WESTERN PENNSYLVANIA HOMESTEAD
1700s**

91

Nicholas Dawson
1745 – 1789

Marched, Nicholas in a long Dawson line.
Montgomery County Maryland. Hundred year,
Or more, his forebears there, where they incline,
To stay put. But Nick would lead, not arrear.

West-pushing masses streaming past his door.
Grabbed up Vallette, their kids. Sold off his all.
Nick on the ground, dead, hundred miles no more,
Ancestral hearths. Vallette must make the call.

Walked on west, with but half her brood. Did not,
Delay the search for their new dad; found one.
Picked local boy, the good Solomon Scott.
Who Knew? Their granddaughter wed Nick's grandson.

Vicissitudes of time need not us wreck.
The unexpected death we might expect.

OLIVER SWAINE TAYLOR, M.D.

92

Oliver Swaine Taylor
1784 – 1885

Awareness, not convention, took Swaine far.
His father wanted Swaine to work the farm.
Each book Swaine read illumined a bright star,
Swaine might reach if he stretched a bit his arm.

Was brain, not brawn that lifted Swaine above.
To Swaine, Dartmouth its highest honors gave.
In humankind Swaine found his deepest love.
Obsessive doc, Swaine would all patients save.

As teacher, Swaine earned national renown.
As preacher, Swaine beseeched high morals keep.
In old age, Swaine taught pris'ners in his town.
Swaine at one hundred died in peaceful sleep.

Skilled Oliver Swaine Taylor, splendid man.
Improved upon each work that he began.

PATRICK HENRY

93

Patrick Henry
1736 – 1799

From Border lands they came to claim a place,
In furth'est reaches of the royal realm.
Scots Irish, coming poor was no disgrace.
Proud, clannish, they'd, the Red Coats, overwhelm.

Parliament overreach, they frowned upon.
To fight and 'haps to die caused them no balk.
Treat "lowland troubles" with the musket balm.
King barred them from the West? An end to talk!

The Henrys and the Winstons lead the fight.
Railed, rallied neighbors, honored yet the king.
These borderers enraged, when might trumps right.
Said: might serves right, free people's freedoms ring.

Think cousin Patrick's views were some extreme?
Cut off the grasping hand! No in between!

CECILIUS CALVERT
2ND BARON BALTIMORE
1605 - 1675

94

Robert Doyne
? – 1689

Poor Robert Doyne, his death by no means earned.
Bob came young to proprietary ground.
Or, raised in Maryland, retired, returned.
His qualities applauded all around.

High sheriff, his wife from the gov'nor's home.
Bought grand estates, astute in churchly choice.
He C of E, while brother looked to Rome.
Two Irish boys, raised money and not voice.

Life in his reins, then wife dead, he fell ill.
None could fathom his terrible contort.
A clerk assisted Bob compose his will.
He died before he signed; they rushed to court.

Comes life then death to each and all the same.
Control and command no part of the game.

THE *DOVE*
(reconstructed)

95

Sarah Scott Baldwin
1791 – 1817

A sample, bit of cloth, to mark her years.
Precise: "In Memory of S Baldwin
1817" doubtless prompted tears,
From the small seamstress daughter, who called in,

Her father, to approve her careful work.
But nine, Jane thus evoked her absent mum,
In simple fabric and her handiwork.
Framed rag, calls both to mind, centuries come.

Dear Sarah, ancient, ever young mother.
Barred from her little ones, world without end.
Longs not for own missed life but another,
Child weeping, cloth and needle in her hand.

You, Sarah, we recall while we have breath.
Pray for us now and in the hour of death.

96

Sarah Stebbens Parsons
1686 – 1758

Poor Sarah Stebbens' sorrows had no cease.
Both parents dead before this child reached ten.
By stepmother raised on, her woes increase.
Her hearth mastered by older kids, not kin.

She married David Parsons, prospects bright.
A parsons' wife, was parson's wife two ways.
He took a church, then second, aimed for height,
Of prestige, based on promise elders made.

The promise chimeral, the income too.
Dave went to court. No church would have him then.
Pariahs they became, their friends were few.
Her hopes for peaceful hearth destroyed again.

Refused, this parson, churchyard for his bones.
As through her life, dead Sarah all alone.

KENTUCKY CABIN, EARLY 19TH CENTURY

97

Solomon Scott
? – ?

Sound Solomon comes plain in others' tales.
In self-cast light, a shadowed silhouette.
Glimpsed in Wellsville on pioneering trails,
Wed a fresh widow. Sol her kids did get.

With her, went west to Blue Lick in K Y.
Her Elenor picked out young William Moore.
Anglican Mom Valette: no knot they'll tie,
Without a priest. Good Sol took up the chore,

To find one, bring him back for his Valette.
Sol next seen, in Ohio, in Springfield.
His daughter Sarah, Jonah Baldwin gets.
Their Jane weds son of Elenor and Will.

The ordinary chores, gallant appear,
In men like Solly, steady year on year.

SIR THOMAS ELYOT

98

Sir Thomas Elyot
c. 1490 – 1546

Knighted, Sir Thomas Elyot, after dawn,
O'er England 'rose, bright, hefty Tudor sun.
Though rays yet faint, entrenched Dark Ages gone.
Elyot, thoughtful, humane. Mind's time begun,

In him. Said, of children a disaster,
Use whips and rods. From monkish wisdom culled.
Tom wrote, blows by "cruel and irous Master"
Young forms bruised and "wits of children be dulled."

Sage Elyot could not save young Barnaby,
When boy-king Edward VI did boyish wrong.
Whipping Boy was wanted; spanked 'cross the knee
Of courtiers, fearful to hit their sov'reign.

Erasmus and Elyot would schools reform.
Their schemes delayed. Pray end to night! Come morn!

99

Thomas Moore
1745 – 1823

Sure, Thomas Moore walked with them stride for stride.
Wed Mary Harrison, his compass set.
The Pennsylvanians fought, took Virgin's side.
State borders finally made, hard feelings yet.

Will Harrison and Ben, in-laws' repute
And fire gave Tom support and had his back,
In each and every fight and armed dispute,
Tom walked with them in backwoods, track for track.

Revolt against the Brits, that freed the West,
For settl'rs. Ben and Thomas early went.
Marked out Kentucky lands they liked the best.
With Mary, Tom worked farm, thought Heaven sent.

Marry your dream girl, make your dreams come true.
Marry Mary, marry Mary's clan, too.

OLD AUGUSTA HOMESTEAD, 1805

100

William Baldwin
1716 – 1786

Will Baldwin, a natural force appears.
Had energy to spare, but not to waste.
On Pennsylvania seaboard, spent long years.
Wed, raised a large family, showed no haste.

Some prompt, this elder citizen received.
Took leave of Chester, with land grant inscribed.
When found in old Augusta, no doubt pleased,
To stop there with a young wife by his side.

Jane but twenty-one, Will, fifty-seven.
She bore him seven kids, a good amount.
All raised C of E, their route to Heaven.
Those left in Chester, 'nother seven count.

Will's new commandment for farm and for life:
Love not thy neighbor; love thou well thy wife.

**AFRICANS
LANDING AT JAMESTOWN
1619**

101

William Cotton
c. 1600 – 1640

Bill Cotton holy orders took at home.
Sent west by Bishop; mold the virgin clay.
In Nassau stopped. Bill, dusky flesh enthroned.
Two negroes to Virginia, where they'd pray.

Got land for bringing three extra, not five.
Domingo and Sambo, the names passed down.
Men honored, one by Sabbath, one by Jive.
Poor Bill died, when a vicarage just found.

Named Mingo and Sam, chattel in Bill's will.
Their fate well known, though unmarked in the book,
That chronicles brave deeds, heroic skill.
New Old Dominion slaves. Honor mistook.

Full fettered men, their own bequest quite plain.
To owners, wealth; death to themselves; Brits, shame.

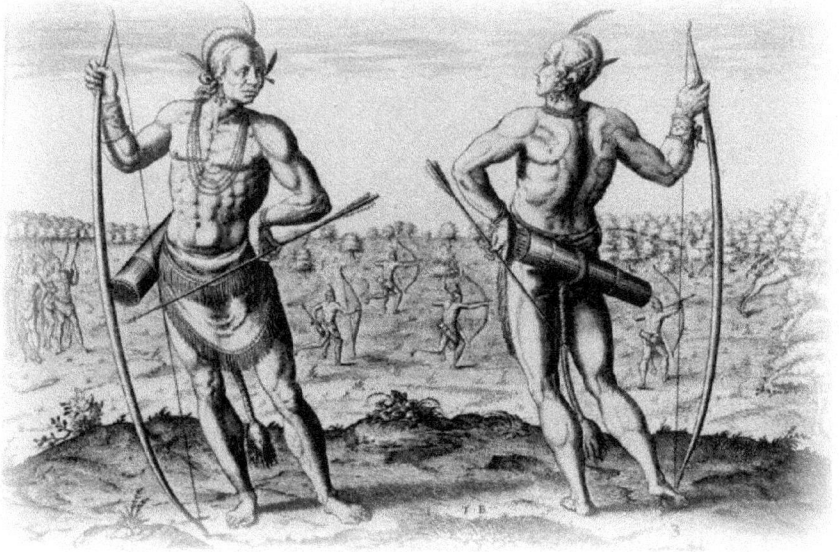

INDIANS IN VIRGINIA, 1585

102

William Harrison
? – 1782

Will Harrison had good, then real bad luck.
Frontier land deals with brother Benjamin.
For Will, good, as Ben never passed the buck.
Ever. But Will was never seen again,

When he walked with Crawford to Sandusky,
Against the Shawnee, who waited, prepared.
The Whites looked forward to a kill party.
The Shawnee, fighting for their lives, each shared,

A desperate rage. Well armed, backs to the wall,
Militia farm boys sent in wild-eyed flight.
The ones they didn't cut, shoot, kill or maul,
Or torture, naked, with fire, day and night.

Will Harrison, the chance is pretty slim,
Recalled for what he did, not did to him.

103

William Hathorne
1606/7 - 1681

Young Will Hathorne came bold, with Book and sword.
A "sable-cloaked, progenitor" was he.
Nathaniel's words (not mine), which do record
The Will who killed, when not on bended knee.

From England to here, lugged foul urge to judge,
The faith and thoughts of others. Very cause,
Of his own flight. But now his motives smudged.
When persecuted persecutes, we pause,

Reflecting on the irony of life.
Insisting freedom was for very few,
Created, William Hathorne, needless strife.
For us, near lost chance to make world anew.

Our luck, accepting Madison's wise creed.
America was born in word, then deed.

104

William Moore
1780 - 1859

Will Moore, who benefitted more than most.
Child of the grandest deeds, Patriots wrought.
Neglected not his heritage, to boast.
Gave home the battle name, where father fought.

Born in P A, child on Kentucky farm,
His father claimed then carved out of the wood.
Wed Elenor at Blue Lick. Did no harm,
Folks had Ohio ties, where first home stood.

Moved back soon to Kentucky, raised nine kids.
Lived there in quiet gentlemanly grace.
Blessed with large lands, family, long life, 'midst
Those slaves, who worked the hardest 'round his place.

Reasons unstated when farm boys jump south.
Free labor's cheaper; notion best unmouth.

**KING CHARLES I
OF ENGLAND, SCOTLAND, ETC.
1600 – 1649**

105

William Stone
1595/6 – 1660

Virginian William Stone put folks at ease.
By Puritans admired and – scope expand –
The Catholics. Was C of E, but pleased,
To help the Calverts. Moved to Maryland.

Govern for them. Brought wife and property:
"Four negroes, one Indian, and one Turk"
All went well until Cromwell thought that he,
Would make M D a Puritanic work.

Two quite small armies on the Severn met.
Will Stone was wounded, had to end the fight.
Lucinda, on his freedom, her cap set.
Succeeded. Will bid history good night.

Milton: "Perhaps their loves or else their sheep,
That did their silly thoughts so busy keep."

PLYMOUTH BAY IN WINTER, 1620

106

William Walton
1605 - 1668

Did William Walton commend men to God?
We check old records, which uncertain be.
The faintest paths in England show Will trod,
Routes of unmastered Pilgrims, to be free.

With two degrees from Cambridge in his cap,
Will Walton in a Seaton pastorate.
No sign there of ejection or mishap,
Our William yet migrated from that state.

Arrived in Boston, 1635
With pinched pocketbook. William always strove,
For funds, that 'Lizbeth and their nine might thrive.
Church duties, Will forsook, ran Jeffrey's Cove.

Grim Pills censure conduct, cite Holy Writ.
What business at the Cove did they permit?

ILLUSTRATIONS

Sonnet 1 – Photo, posted August 31, 2009 at Old Picture of the Day
http://old-photos.blogspot.com/2009/08/country-church.html
Sonnet 2 – Photo – *Historical magazine of Monongahela's old home coming
week*: Sept. 6-13, 1908, p. 232, posted at GoogleBooks
http://books.google.com
Sonnet 3 – Illustration posted at http://karenswhimsy.com/public-domain-
images/vintage-women/vintage-women-1.shtm
Sonnet 4 – Illustration posted at *Public Domain Pics,*
http://www.publicdomainpic.co.cc/2010/09/cannon_26.html
Sonnet 5 – From photo, Portrait by Leah Fanning Mebane, fanningart.com
Sonnet 6 – Illustration No 1 posted at http://www.clker.com/clipart-pig-
outline.html; # 2, *Harpers Weekly* 1877, posted at Wikipedia,
http://en.wikipedia.org/wiki/File:The_Moonshine_Man_of_Kentuc
ky_Harper'sWeekly_1877.jpg
Sonnet 7 – Drawing, *The Saint Bartholomew's Day Massacre 1576*, by François
Dubois (1529–1584) posted at Wikimedia Commons.
http://en.wikipedia.org/wiki/File:Massacre_saint_barthelemy.jpg
Sonnet 8 – Drawing, *History of the Indian Tribes of the United States,* Henry
Rowe Schoolcraft, Part 6 (Philadelphia: Lippincott, 1857), p. 148,
posted at GoogleBooks (books.google.com)
Sonnet 9 – Illustration, *Old book Illustrations* posted at
*http://www.oldbookillustrations.com/pages/woman-holding-
drawing.php?lng=en*
Sonnet 10 – Photo by permission of Carolyn Wickens, on web at
http://www.findagrave.com/cgi-bin/fg.cgi?page=gr&GRid=41477222
Sonnet 11 – From photos, Portraits by Leah Fanning Mebane, fanningart.com
Sonnet 12 – Photo #1 posted at nps.gov; photo #2 posted
athttp://www.findagrave.com/cgi-
bin/fg.cgi?page=gr&GRid=21753245
Sonnet 13 – Photo, digital copy in possession of he author
Sonnet 14 – Portrait posted at Wiki Commons:
http://commons.wikimedia.org/wiki/File:Louis_XIV_of_France.jpg
Sonnet 15 – Photo, A *History of Kentucky and Kentuckians*, E Polk Johnson,
Vol 2 1912, p. 901; posted at GoogleBooks, http://books.google.com
Sonnet 16 – Photo, *The Architecture of Colonial America,* Harold Donaldson
Eberlein (Boston: Little Brown, 1915) pp. 4-5, posted at GoogleBooks
http://books.google.com
Sonnet 17 – Hubble Spiral, NASA photo
Sonnet 18 – Photo, *Cosmopolitan Magazine*, Vol 22, 1896-97, p. 663, posted at
GoogleBooks http://books.google.com
Sonnet 19 – Illustration posted at pdclipart.org
http://www.pdclipart.org/displayimage.php?album=50&pos=19
Sonnet 20 – Photo, courtesy of Carolyn Wickens
Sonnet 21 – Photo, *Shenandoah Valley Pioneers and Their Descendants: A
history of Frederick*, Thomas Kemp Cartmell, (1908, p. 222) Posted
at GoogleBooks http://books.google.com
Sonnet 22 – *Last Judgment*, Jean Cousin the Younger, also called Jehan Cousin
Le Jeune (c. 1522–1595) posted at Wikimedia
Sonnet 23 – Photo, posted at blogspot.com,
http://freshpics.blogspot.com/2007/05/beautiful-lightning-
pictures.html

Sonnet 24 – Photo, *Shenandoah Valley Pioneers and Their Descendants: A history of Frederick*, Thomas Kemp Cartmell, (1908, p. 252) Posted at GoogleBooks http://books.google.com

Sonnet 25 – Illustration posted at Clker.com; http://www.clker.com/clipart-15127.html

Sonnet 26 – From photo, Portrait by Leah Fanning Mebane, fanningart.com

Sonnet 27 – Illustration, *"My Old Kentucky Home"*, Stephen Foster (Boston, Ticknor and Company, 1888) Illustration by Mary Hallock Foote and Charles Copeland

Sonnet 28 – Photo 1, "The Face of Slavery," http://www.photographymuseum.com/faceof.html Photo 2, Barber- Scotia College website, http://www.b-sc.edu/

Sonnet 29 – From photo, Portrait by Leah Fanning Mebane, fanningart.com

Sonnet 30 – From Old Book Illustrations, http://www.oldbookillustrations.com/pages/wistful.php?lng=en

Sonnet 31 – From *Public Domain Photos, Landscapes*, http://www.public-domain-photos.com/landscapes/sky/sunrise-3-free-stock-photo-4.htm

Sonnet 32 – Illustration from http://www.clker.com/clipart-2412.html

Sonnet 33 – Photo, *Historical magazine of Monongahela's old home coming week*: Sept. 6-13, 1908, p. 110, posted at GoogleBooks http://books.google.com

Sonnet 34 – From photo, Portrait by Leah Fanning Mebane, fanningart.com

Sonnet 35 – Photo, *Big Bone Gardens*, http://www.big-bone-gardens.com/big-bone-gardens-in-the-snow/#more-104

Sonnet 36 – Photo, *Old Photos*, http://old-photos.blogspot.com/search/label/Ships

Sonnet 37 – Photo placed on floodfamily.org by Ron Wagner

Sonnet 38 – Photo posted at http://www.arlingtoncemetery.net/mwireland.htm

Sonnet 39 – Illustration posted at http://www.oldbookillustrations.com/pages/boneset.php?lng=en

Sonnet 40 – Painting, after Leonardo da Vinci, *La Scapigliata* via the Web Gallery of Art

Sonnet 41 – Illustration posted at http://karenswhimsy.com/public-domain-images/tree-silhouettes/tree-silhouettes-3.shtm

Sonnet 42- Illustration posted at http://www.wpclipart.com/American_History/pastimes_and_fashion/early_Dutch_dress.png.html

Sonnet 43 – From photo, Portrait by Leah Fanning Mebane, fanningart.com

Sonnet 44 – From photo, Portrait by Leah Fanning Mebane, fanningart.com

Sonnet 45 – Photo, *The Architecture of Colonial America*, Harold Donaldson Eberlein (Boston: Little Brown, 1915) pp. 4-5, posted at GoogleBooks http://books.google.com

Sonnet 46 – Photo, Endrtimes.blogspot http://endrtimes.blogspot.com/2008/02/it-is-growing-custom-to-narrow-control.html

Sonnet 47 – Illustration taken from the *Dictionnaire encyclopédique Trousset*, also known as the *Trousset encyclopedia*, Paris, 1886 – 1891, on the web at Old Book Illustrations, http://www.oldbookillustrations.com/pages/orchid1.php?lng=en

Sonnet 48 – Photo posted at Wikimedia Commons, http://commons.wikimedia.org/wiki/File:Cicatrices_de_flagellation_sur_un_esclave.jpg

Sonnet 49 – "Alone" by Dulac (*The Poetical Works of Edgar Alan Poe,* illustrated by Edmund Dulac, 1921) posted at kerenswhimsey.com

Sonnet 50 – "The Virgin at the Loom," *The Graphic*, Dec 14, 1901, p. 796

Sonnet 51 – Drawing, *Nicotiana tabacum* posted by Southwest School of Botanical Medicine, Bisbee, AZ, posted at http://www.swsbm.com/Illustrations/Nicotiana_tabacum.gif

Sonnet 52 – *Twin Oaks*, posted at kerenswhimsey.com, http://karenswhimsy.com/tree-silhouettes.shtm

Sonnet 53 – Photo, *The Architecture of Colonial America*, Harold Donaldson Eberlein (Boston: Little Brown, 1915) p. 60, posted at GoogleBooks http://books.google.com

Sonnet 54 – From photo, Portrait by Leah Fanning Mebane, fanningart.com

Sonnet 55 – From photo, Portrait by Leah Fanning Mebane, fanningart.com

Sonnet 56 - Photo, Bliss home, courtesy, *Connecticut Valley Historical Museum, Springfield, MA* http://larkturnthehearts.blogspot.com/2007/11/early-america-mary-bliss-parsons.html

Sonnet 57 – Photo, P*ortrait and Biographical Record of Denver and Vicinity* (Chapman Publishing Company Chicago 1898) Mardos Collection, posted at www.memoriallibrary.com/CO/1898DenverPB/

Sonnet 58 – Harvard College from Early American Images, http://www.earlyamericanimages.com/places1.html

Sonnet 59 – Wood engraving, from *L'illustration*, 1 August 1857 (no 753), portrait of Frédéric Sauvage by Gavarni

Sonnet 60 – *Female silhouette*, posted at kerenswhimsey.com http://karenswhimsy.com/female-silhouette.shtm

Sonnet 61 – *The Underworld*, image posted by at "Visual by www.PDImages.com" at http://www.pdimages.com/X0010.html-ssi

Sonnet 63 – Photo posted at *Public Domain Clip Art*, http://www.pdclipart.org/displayimage.php?album=47&pos=2

Sonnet 64 –Illustration, "Capture of the Indian Fortress," *King Philip, Sovereign Chief of the Wampanoags: The Early History of The Settlers of New England*, John C. Abbott (New York: Harpers and Brothers, 1857, p. 247, at Google Books, *Googlebooks.com*

Sonnet 65 – Image at *Public Domain Clip Art*, http://www.pdclipart.org/displayimage.php?album=150&pos=24

Sonnet 66 – Image, Stipple engraving by J.P. Simon, 1810, posted at *Res Obscura*, http://resobscura.blogspot.com/2010/07/witchcraft-and-magic-images-from.html

Sonnet 68 -From photos, Portraits by Leah Fanning Mebane, fanningart.com

Sonnet 69 – Portrait of Madison, posted at http://www.shmoop.com/constitution/photo-james-madison-portrait.html and http://commons.wikimedia.org/wiki/File:James_Madison.jpg

Sonnet 70 – Photo, *Historical magazine of Monongahela's old home coming week*: Sept. 6-13, 1908, p. -107, posted at GoogleBooks http://books.google.com

Sonnet 71 – From photos, Portraits by Leah Fanning Mebane, fanningart.com

Sonnet 72 – Photo posted at Wiki Commons, http://en.wikipedia.org/wiki/File:President-Jefferson-Davis.jpg

Sonnet 73 –Painting by G.H. Boughton, posted at http://standingonshoulders.net/

Sonnet 74 – Photo, *History of North Carolina*, Vol 2, William Boyd, New York: Lewis Publishing 1919, p. 188, on line at GoogleBooks http://books.google.com

Sonnet 75 – Photo posted at *Women in History* blog,
        http://womenhistory.blogspot.com/2007_10_01_archive.html
Sonnet 76 – From photo, Portrait by Leah Fanning Mebane, fanningart.com
Sonnet 77 – From photos, Portraits by Leah Fanning Mebane, fanningart.com
Sonnet 78 – photo, *Parsons Family* by Henry Parsons (New York: Alaban
        Genealogical Company, 1912), p. 42, posted at GoogleBooks
        http://books.google.com
Sonnet 79 – Drawing, http://publicdomainclip-art.blogspot.com
        /2010/10/witchcraft-trial-at-salem-village.html and at Wikipedia,
        SalemWitchcraftTrial.jpg; photo, *Israel Putnam*, William F.
        Livingston (New York: G.P. Putnam & Sons, pp. 2-3), posted at
        GoogleBooks http://books.google.com
Sonnet 80 – Photo posted at carthage.lib.il.us
Sonnet 81 – From photo, Portrait by Leah Fanning Mebane, fanningart.com
Sonnet 82 – From photo, Portrait by Leah Fanning Mebane, fanningart.com
Sonnet 83 – From photos, Portraits by Leah Fanning Mebane, fanningart.com
Sonnet 84 – Illustration, posted at
        http://homepages.rootsweb.ancestry.com/~sam/bliss/mary.html
Sonnet 85 – Illustration, *History of the Indian Tribes of the United States*,
        Henry Rowe Schoolcraft (Philadelphia: Lippincott, 1857) page 664,
        posted at GoogleBooks http://books.google.com
Sonnet 88 – Family photo
Sonnet 89 – Photo 1, "Log Cabin in Winter, posted at Public Domain Clip Art,
        http://publicdomainclip-art.blogspot.com/2009/01/log-cabin-in-
        winter.html
        Photo 2, "Surfing on Ocean," Public-Domain-Image.com/surfing,
        http://public-domain-image.com/sport-public-domain-images-
        pictures/surfing;"Surfing on ocean" by Jon Sullivan
Sonnet 90 – Photo, U S History Images, http://ushistoryimages.com/valley-
        forge.shtm
Sonnet 91 – Photo, *Historical magazine of Monongahela's old home coming*
        week: Sept. 6-13, 1908, p. 45, posted at GoogleBooks
        http://books.google.com
Sonnet 92 – Photo, No 6 (No 438) *The Phrenological Journal* (No 60 "Whole
        Number 438") (*Life Illustrated*) June 1875, p. 355, posted at
        GoogleBooks http://books.google.com
Sonnet 93 – Portrait posted at American Revolutionary War,
        http://americanrevwar.homestead.com/files/henry.htm
Sonnet 94 – Portrait by Florence MacKubin (1861-1918), posted at Wikimedia
        Commons, Calvertcecil.jpg; Photo, posted at Wikimedia Commons,
        Maryland Dove.jpg
Sonnet 95 – Illustration, posted at kerenswhimsey.com -
        http://karenswhimsy.com/silhouettes-of-people.shtm
Sonnet 96 – Illustration, *The Scarlet Letter,* Nathaniel Hawthorne, New York:
        Doubleday & McClure Co, 1898, pp. 300-01, posted at GoogleBooks
        http://books.google.com
Sonnet 97 – Photo, *History of Kentucky, Vol 4,* By William Elsey Connelley,
        Ellis Merton Coulter (New York, Chicago: American Historial Society,
        1922) p. 42
Sonnet 98 – Drawing by Holbein, posted at Wikimedia Commons
        http://commons.wikimedia.org/wiki/Main_Page
Sonnet 99 – Illustration, *The Deerslayer*, James Fenamore Cooper (Boston,
        New York: Houghton Mifflin, 1876, 1898) p. 404, posted at
        GoogleBooks http://books.google.com

Sonnet 100 – Photo, *Historical magazine of Monongahela's old home coming week*: Sept. 6-13, 1908, p. 56, posted at GoogleBooks http://books.google.com

Sonnet 101 – Illustration posted at PBS.org. http://www.pbs.org/wgbh/aia/part1/1h289.html

Sonnet 102 – Engraving by Theodore de Bry, 1590, based on a 1585 watercolor by John White, posted by schmoop.com, *Jamestown & Early Colonial Virginia* http://www.shmoop.com

Sonnet 103 – Illustration, *The House of the Seven Gables,* Volume 2, Nathaniel Hawthorne, illustrations by Maude Alice Cowles and Genevieve Cowles, (Boston, New York: Houghton Mifflin, 1876, 1898) p.202, posted at GoogleBooks http://books.google.com

Sonnet 104 – Photo, The American Museum of Photography, *The Face of Slavery*, http://www.photographymuseum.com/uncleboblg.html

Sonnet 105 – Portrait by Anthony van Dyck, 1636, posted at http://en.wikipedia.org/wiki/Charles_I_of_England

Sonnet 106 – Illustration, wpclipart.com, *Plymouth bay in winter 1620*, at http://www.wpclipart.com/American_History/settlement/Plymouth/Plymouth_bay_in_winter_1620.png.html

www.ingramcontent.com/pod-product-compliance
Lightning Source LLC
Chambersburg PA
CBHW031833090426
42741CB00005B/228